Face-to-Face
with
The Cat

Stéphane Frattini

Photos by Jean-Louis Klein and
Marie-Luce Hubert of the BIOS Agency

ini Charlesbridge

2

Large yards and gardens make excellent hunting grounds for cats.

Curious critters

Cats are independent animals. They prowl through gardens and backyards, exploring every nook and cranny. Cats are also curious creatures. They sniff familiar odors, but when they smell an unfamiliar scent cats mark their territories with a small bit of urine. This marking lets other cats know that the territory is taken.

Cats sit in high perches, such as trees, to get a better view of their surroundings.

Well equipped

Cats have 600 muscles that allow them to twist and turn in many ways. They have flexible ears and can isolate one sound among many, even sounds that are far away.

They have pointed canine teeth. Their claws are protected by cushions, or pads, when not in use. Their whiskers act as antennae, helping cats find their way at night.

 Cats' eyes adjust to the light. If it is shady, their pupils are large and open.

Cats wash themselves with long strokes of their tongues. Their rough tongues make cleaning fur easy.

When it is bright, cats' pupils contract until they are just slits.

Cats' claws are retractable, meaning a cat can make them go in and out.

Cats become alert when they hear sounds.

They meet

Mature male cats are called tomcats. When it is mating time, tomcats will wander around for several days in search of female cats.

 *Females that are ready to mate are said to be "in heat." Cats in heat emit odors to attract male cats.*

Males will wrestle and meow loudly to get the attention of females in heat.

By scratching, males alert females that they are marking the females' territories.

Tomcats will travel long distances to find female cats.

The largest, strongest tomcat chases the other cats away. He will be the father of the female's kittens. Excited, with her tail in the air, she meows loudly and rubs up against the places where the male has left his scent.

Kittens are born!

After mating, female cats shoo male cats away. Male cats do not help raise kittens. Nine weeks later, females are ready to give birth. Owners can prepare a basket, but most female cats find their own quiet birthing places, such as barns.

Kittens need time to get used to people. Never force kittens to be held.

 Mother cats nurse their kittens for one month. There is a teat for each kitten, which they find by scent. Mother cats purr to make kittens feel secure.

One by one, kittens are born headfirst. Mother cats will bathe and feed their kittens and keep them close for warmth.

 Kittens' eyes open after 8 days. All kittens are born with blue eyes.

Playtime

At about three weeks, kittens begin playing together. Each kitten has its own personality. Some are shy, and some are bossy. After one month, they explore their surroundings and discover familiar sounds and scents. Mother cats keep watchful eyes on their kittens. If kittens cry, their mothers quickly come to their aid and bring them back to their baskets.

An average litter has 4 or 5 kittens, but the record is 12!

Cats transport kittens in their mouths, holding them by the skin of their necks. This does not hurt the kittens.

 Kittens will climb furniture, but being small they have trouble getting down again.

 Yarn and other toys keep kittens playing for hours.

🐈 *Kittens eat about 4 small meals a day.*

🐈 *They chase anything that moves!*

🐈 *When it is bedtime, kittens will cuddle with their owners.*

Buddies!

Kittens need company. They get bored if left on their own. That is why sisters and brothers make great playmates.

After nursing for one month, kittens can eat meat. Kittens have to learn to share food since they usually share a dish. They sleep a lot, 16 hours a day, often snuggling together.

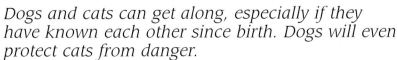

Dogs and cats can get along, especially if they have known each other since birth. Dogs will even protect cats from danger.

Super sensitive

When kittens are two months old, they are nervous and jump at the slightest noise. Cats can hear higher-pitched sounds than humans. They also learn to communicate with scents. When they are near unfamiliar people or objects, cats always sniff them first. Once a scent is registered, cats remember it for their entire lives.

Thanks to a small duct between the nose and the palate, a cat's sense of smell is 1,000 times greater than a human's.

A little kiss from Mom is also a chance to exchange reassuring scents.

Whack! Kittens often scuffle to see who is the strongest.
Real fights are rare and quickly forgotten.

🐾 *Ovens and laundry machines can be dangerous to curious kittens and should never be left open.*

🐾 *When threatened or angry, cats spit and fold back their ears.*

Cats are very clean and easily learn how to use litter boxes.

If cats burn themselves once, they will stay away from fire in the future.

Live and learn

Kittens learn from experience. If bees sting them, then kittens will be more careful the next time they sniff flowers. Inside the house, the dangers are greater. Kittens find out that candles, radiators, and stovetops can burn their paws. After being scolded by owners four or five times, kittens begin to obey when their owners say "no."

17

 When hunting, cats silently sneak up on their prey, their bellies low and their gazes fixed.

With a quick smack of their paw, cats capture their prey.

Cats divide their living spaces into areas for hunting, mating, play, and rest.

Cats proudly bring home their kills to their owners. They are looking for praise and get confused when scolded for this behavior.

Super hunters

At first, mother cats bring food to their kittens. Soon kittens are ready to hunt alone. Mice, birds, or large insects—everything that moves becomes prey. They creep forward, their bodies low to the ground. Suddenly, they leap at their prey, claws first. One in four times, cats succeed in catching their prey. Imagine how much a whole litter can catch!

Adoption

When kittens are three months old, they are ready to be adopted. At first, kittens may be shy or hide from their new owners, but soon enough they find toys to play with. By rubbing their scent on their new owners' legs, kittens are asking to be petted. Owning a cat is a big responsibility, so it is important to learn how to care for it.

 Cats are independent animals that need moments of freedom.

Cats often get attached to one person.

A modest friend

Over 5,000 years ago, the Egyptians tamed cats so that they would catch mice. Today cats are everywhere. If you want to raise healthy cats, you should learn how to take care of them. With enough love, care, and attention, cats can become great companions.

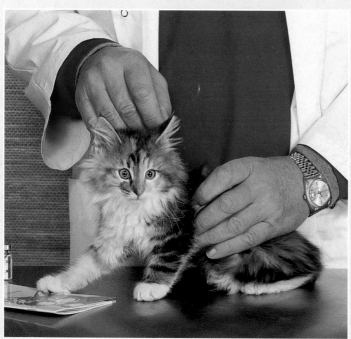

 Bright eyes and warm noses are signs of healthy cats.

Caring for your cat

There are over 75 million cats in the United States. Cats should be brought to the veterinarian once a year, especially if they are outdoor cats. Like humans, cats need to be vaccinated against diseases and viruses. Flea collars are a good idea for outdoor cats. Name tags with owners' names and addresses help identify lost cats. Healthy indoor cats can live up to 15 to 20 years.

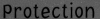

Controlling the cat population

Stray cats often pose problems. In cities they make a racket, and in the country they kill birds and can carry rabies. Vets can spay or neuter cats so that they cannot reproduce. This helps control the cat population and makes for healthier cats in the future.

Good companions

Cats are ideal pets for children and elderly people. Gentle and affectionate, cats are easier to care for than dogs because cats are independent. Also, petting a cat can be calming and soothing for humans. The only difficulty is that some people are allergic to cat saliva, which is found on their fur.

Cats are faithful companions for lonely people.

23

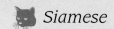 *Siamese*

Breeds of cats

Today there are more than 60 breeds of domestic cats. Humans have created other hybrids by crossbreeding cats. Most breeds fall into two categories: longhaired and shorthaired.

Siamese cats have sleek silhouettes and triangular heads. They are noted for their voices and can be chatty. Siamese get attached to their owners and will follow them wherever they go.

Maine coons are the giants of cats. They can weigh as much as 18 pounds! Native to the cold forests of North America, they have long, thick fur, which protects them from harsh winters. Maine coons can be trained to fetch small objects.

 Maine coon

24

Persians are the best known of pedigreed cats. They are easily recognized by their square heads, pug noses, and long fur.

Sphynx are hairless cats! They first came into being by a fluke of nature, but then a breed was created. Sweet but delicate, Sphynx fear the cold as well as the strong sunlight.

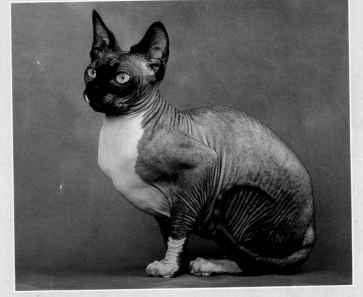

 Sphynx

25

Here are some questions about the lives of the cats. You will find the answers in your book.

Photograph credits:

BIOS Agency: All photographs by J.-L. Klein and M.-L. Hubert except: M. Gunther: pp. 2–3, p. 6 (bottom); C. Ruoso: p. 7 (top); J.-J. Étienne: p. 4 (bottom); F. Vidal: p. 12 (bottom left), p. 16 (top); J.-L. Ziegler: p. 17 (top), p. 4 (top), p. 5 (top left); H. Ausloos: pp. 16–17 (bottom), p. 25 (top); Gayo: p. 5 (bottom); F. Mordel: pp. 18–19 (bottom); N. Reinhard/Okapia: p. 19 (top); N. Petit: p. 23 (bottom); M. Nicolotti: p. 24 (top).